Cartographies of Absence

Cartographies of Absence

Mahmoud Al-Zayed

Adroit Publishers
NEW DELHI • KATHMANDU

ISBN : 978-81-87393-64-1

Arabic Title: *Ala Khara't al-ghiyab*

Published by
ADROIT PUBLISHERS
4675/21, Ganpati Bhawan, Ansari Road,
Daryaganj, New Delhi-110 002 Phone : 011-23266030
adroitpublishers@gmail.com

Editorial Assistance (English) – Tanmoyee Rajkhowa
Jacket Design – Sukruti Anah Stanley
Arabic Calligraphy – Ahmad K. Ghrouz

All paintings used in the cover as well as inside the book are adaptations of the original paintings done by the artist Jonathan Varghese

Typeset in Garamond & Traditional Arabic by Arun, Akriti Graphic Solution, Delhi-110081 E-mail: arun263923@gmail.com, Ph: 9999414390

Printed at Thomson Press India Limited

"I desire nothing from love but art, and if it comes from absence, then absence is love"

Mustafa Sadiq al-Rafii

For my parents, Mohammad and Fatima,
Anuradha Ghosh,

And for her, a cartographer of absence,
I utter her name in silence

M

Contents

Preface

Her presence near the window while the rays of the sun light insinuated through her dark-blonde hair with which she was playing, waiting for me to offer her a cup of coffee, 'the gateway to you, a mysterious cave,' thus she used to say – which I used to hand over to her every morning around 8 o'clock. The scene appeared differently from the other side: a portrait of a full-lit window obstructed by her dark shadow. The off-blue wall ornamented by carelessly hanged portraits of late ones completed the whole picture. I, on the other hand, never told her, among many other things, that her morning presence was the key to my day. Now her absence is fully completed only through my presence, manifested in one's morning cup of coffee, surrounded by jasmine flowers, in a pure Damascene morning. Regardless of absence and separation, nonetheless, she was (hopefully is) always waiting for me at the end of the road of love, of death, an absence waiting at the receiving end of presence.

The cup of coffee would spur her first thoughts of a poem to come. She writes some lines and looks at me presenting a smile, a small gift that has the potential to sustain me. The sense of my dependency on her smile always remains mysterious at a time of seemingly constant association with anger, which is partly because of the absurdity of events encircling one's existence and partly out of the sense of helplessness on the face of such events.

The ugly wars – all sorts of wars that persist in attempting to squash one's being – remain the framework of one's life. The continual rapid changes and predicaments that punctuate one's life during these wars, witnessing helplessly the repetitive displacements, and the slow loss of everything one loves and is/was familiar with, forms the collage of the background of one's relentless anger. Though she always felt the unspoken/unsayable, she had never asked me about these wars. What she used to do when she felt that it was getting too much was to leave me alone. Every time she did so, she spelled her resonating word, repeating it thrice: 'write, write, write'. . .

Thus these poems were written at a time of multiple rifts within one's self and between the self and the world, as an attempt to heal an unhealable wound, letting the wound speak for itself, trying to find cure from its own abyss, restructuring the chaos of the times – past and future – and making an inventory of the fragments of the disintegrated absencing selves, bodies, words and worlds, lingering around (a) present body/ies, making a history of their own, a history made out of the ashes of memory, hidden among the words, voids, silences, blank spaces, ellipses, commas, caesuras, and etceteras. The moment of the present – if there is such a thing – is captured by the monumentality of these poems, registering a record of the past, yet in images. To write is to dare to find the missing fragments of the self that are trapped in one's body and (an)other body/ies–a helpless attempt to feel one's being as a whole, yearning to fill the void.

In the dialectics of absence and presence, the absent remains the obstinate being, altering the present one. What is absent from the self, constitutes the interior of what is present. These poems, as my friend Shakeel Anjum would love to write, encounter the abysses and absences of places, and people, staging themselves vis-à-vis a looming death. The texture of the text, fragmented as it were, is like a dismembered body laid in solitude, waiting to be put together and buried like a life that dares to declare itself complete and over. The texts are epigraphs of absent images, times, bodies, verses, traces, stories that are being violently eradicated from one's world. These absences resist the constant act of burying them in oblivion. The book is an attempt to map out these absences, marking the traces of the texts, and one's only wish for them is not to survive.

The urgency of the need to write and the existential situation in which these poems were written are by no means the same as in the time of them entering the domain of another language. However, the space of writing is, like that of translation, the space of the in-between. The moment of writing as such is gone forever, but what remain are the traces in the text, the text that is the manifest of an immanent discourse that one could not render into language with its totality, a stubborn absence. Therefore, all these poems reject any politics of naming – poems with no identity.

Though the phonic musicality of the Arabic text is muted upon entering the domain of the English one, which has its own tonality, the latter is primarily and essentially complementing the former, making harmonious poetic ensembles. This contrapuntal play of Arabic and English texts is staged here vis-à-vis each other as a quest for an unattainable text, a text to come. These poems inhabit the place of the in-between of two languages at least, feeling not right in the house of the languages in which they were written, structuring a house of absence, the text, a form of death, of absence.

Finally, these poems could be read as a *mushaira* between the corpses and the living dead, transfigured in the corpus of this book.

M. Z.
New Delhi
August, 2018

No Text, No Trace

Words bleed from the tips of my fingers
Searching for a being, on the ruined walls
No text, no trace
In a war that lets nothing remain
And leaves nothing unburned. . .

لا نص، لا أَثَر

كلماتٌ تنزف من أطراف أصابعي
تبحث عن ذات لها على حُطام الجُدُر
لا نص، لا أَثَر
في حربٍ لا تبقي و لا تذر . . .

Of Love, Of Death

I have a tremendous desire to see her, my home,
before death, the long lasting absence,
to touch the soil of her body,
to return to the child in one,
to caress her hair with loving hands,
to make time freeze in her presence.

If death is not a constant vigilant watchman of one's
lively life, and if the grammar of life (minus death)
stays unabashed, then one would watch his body
disintegrating slowly (perhaps painfully) in the mirror
of (an)other's being.

To commit suicide is to rush to the conclusion,
declaring the end of the text, jumping over the
beginning and the core body.

عن الحب، عن الموت

لديَّ رغبة هائلة لأن أراها، هي، وطني،
قبل الموت، الغياب الطويل الدائم،
لديَّ رغبةٌ لألمس تراب جسدها،
لأعود لذاك الطفل فيَّ،
لِأُلاطف شعرها بيدي محب،
لأجعل الزمن يتجمَّدُ في حضرتها.

إن لم يكن الموت هو الرَّقيبُ الدَّائمُ الحَذِر على حياة المرءِ الحيَّة،
و إذا كانت قواعد الحياة (عدا الموت) ثابتة،
فما على المرء إلَّا أن يرى جسده يتحللُ رويدًا رويدًا
(ربما بعذابٍ) في مرآة ذاتِ الآخر.

أن تنتحر يعني أن تتسرّعَ للخاتمة معلنًا نهاية النَّص،
متجاوزًا البداية و المتن.

If death is not at the receiving end of life, then life
is of no value.

If she is not absent, then her presence,
that is now indispensable –
like a breath, for a drowning
body besieged and submerged by water, would not be
desired.
To *fall* in love is to have her absence and presence
locked up in a solitary cell in which death and life are
kept handcuffed together.

I know nothing about her, in her absence;
white is the colour of absence,
black is that of presence,
while I have the colour of both and all their shades
in-between.

إذا كان الموت ليس النهاية المستقْبِلةُ للحياة،
فليس ثمَّة معنى لهذه الحياة.

إن لم تكن غائبة، فإن حضورها،
اللَّازم الآن لُزوم نفسٍ لجسمٍ حُوصِرَ و غُمرَ بالماء، لن يكون موضِعَ رغبة.

أن تقع في الحب يعني أن يُحبس غيابها و حضورها في زنزانةٍ انفراديَّةٍ يكون فيها الموت و الحياة مكبَّلي اليدين معًا.

لا أعلم أيَّ شيءٍ عنها في غيابها.
الأبيض هو لون الغياب،
الأسود هو لون الحضور
و أنا هما، تلكما اللونان، و كل الألون بينهما.

5

The Road

Like a stranger
I am pacing on that road
We paced together,
Like strangers.
Now, I do not know the land
I am walking on,
Nor the sky.
The trees are unusually high
Encircling me,
Depriving me of air . . .
I stop behind the shadow
Standing
And wondering
Am I you?
Are you my shadow?
Or I am yours?
Or identical we both are,
At the day and night?

الطريق

كالغريب
أسيرُ في ذاك الطريق
الذي مشيناه معًا
كالغرباء
لا أعرف الأرض
التي أمشي عليها الآن
لا، و لا تلك السّماء
و الأشجار عاليةٌ
تطوقني على غير عادتها
و تحرمني الهواء
و بقيت خلف الظِّل،
ظِلّي، واقفًا
متسائلاً
هل أنا أنتَ؟
هل أنت ظلّي؟
أم أنا ظلُّك؟ أم كلانا في الصبح و في الليل سواء

In that road,
I knew my self
I knew the shadow,
Her shadow,
I am her shadow,
She is the transfiguration. . .

ذاك الطريق به

عرفت نفسي

عرفت الظِّل،

أنا ظِلُّها و هي التجلّي. . .

My Dream

My dream is like a wandering gazelle.
I know her as she knows me.
Whenever I try to catch her,
She escapes from my hand like the wind.
We both are the union of dichotomies,
But she lingers around me like the wind.
Draftily resembling me.
Unbridled I am, just like her.
And she does not believe in time and space,
Just like me.

حلمي

حلمي غزالٌ هائمٌ
أعرفها و تعرفني
كلما حاولت ملك زمامها
فرَّت من يدي كالريح
جمع من الأضداد نحن
و لكنها تبقى معي كالريح،
و تشبهني
أنا مثلها، عصيٌّ أن يُقاد
و لا تؤمن بالزمان و لا المكان، مثلي.

To Die Here or There or In-between: Scene Cipher

Though being besieged by the piles of corpses that surround me, I am striving not to make blood mingled with flesh the habitual scene. If death is the only certain possibility that can punctuate the line of our life at any time, and at any place, then why should I leave the place in which I would love to die?
There is no time left for me to leave. Here I know my grave very well. The soil is familiar to me. I know its fragrance very well. Let me rest here in war, says an old woman seeing her death.
Her lifelong partner says:
I will stay here and rest with her in peace.
A youth says:
This land wraps all its tentacles around my neck. I am almost dead. I have to leave.
A child whose age is some years of war says:
I will not go anywhere for this bag is too cumbersome.

. . . Silence . . .

أن تموت هنا أو هناك أو بين بين: المشهد صفر

في زحمة الجثث التي تحاصرني أحاول جهدي أن لا أجعل خليط الدم واللحم المشهد الإعتيادي. إذا كان الموت هو الاحتمال المؤكد الذي يستطيع أن يقطع خيط الحياة في أي وقت شاء، و في أي مكان شاء، فلماذا أترك المكان الذي أحب أن أموت فيه؟

ليس هناك متسع من الوقت لأرحل. هنا، أعرف قبري جيدًا، ألفتُ تراب هذه الأرض، أعرف عطره جيدًا. دعني أرقد هنا بحرب. كذا تقول امرأة ترى موتها.
سأبقى هنا و أرقد معها بسلام. يقول شريك عمرها.

يقول شاب/ة:
لفَّت الأرض كل أذرعها حول عنقي كأخطبوط. أكاد أموت. لا بد أن أرحل.

يقول طفل بلغ من العمر سبع سنين حرب:
لن أذهب إلى أي مكان فهذه الحقيبة ثقيلة جدًا جدًا.

. . . صَمْت . . .

The Colour of the Dead

The light autumn swallows the heavy leaves of
memories in Berlin.
The sky is grey there and hope is blue . . .
In Delhi, the sky is grey throughout the year.
And in Damascus . . .
In Damascus, the sky forgets all its colours . . .
Was I ever there?
And I am here, in-between,
A dead wearing the mask of the living.
. . .

There is no bread.
What remains is the colour of the dead.
There is no place in the skies.
There is no place in the seas.
There is not even space for a passer-by.
For the skies and the seas are graveyards
And the earth is a coffin.

لون الموتى

الخريف الخفيف يبلع أوراق الذكريات الثقيلة في برلين،
السماء رماديَّةٌ هناك و الأمل أزرق. . .
و في دلهي السَّماء رماديَّةٌ على مدار السَّنة
و في الشَّام. . .
و في الشَّام نَسِيت السَّماءُ ألوانها. . .
أكنت هناك أنا؟
و أنا هنا، بين بين،
ميّتٌ ألبس لَبُوسَ حَيٍّ أنا
. . .

ليس هناك قوت
ليس هناك إلا لون الموتى
لا مكان في السَّماوات
لا مكان في البحار
لا مكان حتى لعابر
فالسَّماوات و البحار مقابر
و الأرض تابوت.

I Am the Obstinate Absence

I fell out of the darkness of love
To the light of misery
I am the substitute, the killed.
. . .

I came out of the space of silence
To the limits of language
I am the fatigued tongue.
. . .

I came out of the innocence of need
To the snare of desire
I am the abject prisoner.
. . .

I broke out of my body
To my self
I am the heavy void.
. . .

أنا الغياب العنيد

خرجتُ من ظُلمةِ الحبّ
إلى نور الشّقاء
أنا البديل القتيل
. . .

خرجت من فضاء الصّمتِ
إلى ضيق اللغة
أنا اللِّسان الكليل
. . .

خرجتُ من براءة الحاجات
إلى شَرَك الرغائب
أنا الأسير الذّليل
. . .

خرجتُ من جسدي
إلى نفسي
أنا الفراغ الثّقيل
. . .

The soul is bored of the sound clay,
Lusting for the distant place
I am the obstinate absence,
The obstinate silence.

مَلَّتِ الروح من صَلْصَالها
تتشهَّى المكان البعيد، البعيد
أنا الغِيابُ العنيد
أنا الصَّمتُ العنيد

Poems I Found Among the Corpses

I am, in the presence of death, killed
And on this earth, I am a wanderer
Searching for a love, deep-rooted,
And like my wounds
This road is long…
. . .

I am robbed of my will, like the one lost in a war.
All those I loved, have departed,
And my heart is burdened with anxieties.
It is not able to endure further. . .
I am overburdened with memories,
Struggling with the waves,
Searching for a rebirth. . .

قصائد وجدتها بين الجثث

أنا في حضرة الموت قتيل
و في الأرض هائمٌ
أبحث عن حبٍ أثيل
و مثل جراحي
هذا الطريق طويل
. . .

كضائعٍ أنا في الحرب مسلوب الإرادة
كل من أحببت غابوا
و القلب لا يقوى جلادة
و مثقلٌ بالذكريات أنا
أجاهد الأمواج
بحثًا عن ولادة. . .

I have some documents the world deems important.

Birth certificate,

A passport that I do not need,

Indispensable?

I passed endless oceans without it

The world condenses my existence in a convenient identity,

Of which I have no control:

My name,

Place and date of birth.

. . .

I am much more than all of this

I am much more than all of this

I am above and beyond all of this.

. . .

و معي أشيائي المهمة:
شهادةُ ميلاد
جواز سفر لا حاجة لي به
لا فكاك منه؟
قطعت بحاراً دونه
العالم يختصر وجودي بهوِيّة
بأشياء لم أختر منها شيئا:
اسمي
مكان الولادة وتاريخها
. . .

أنا أكثر من كل هذا
أنا أكثر من كل هذا
أنا أكثر من كل هذا
. . .

And since I could not choose the place of my birth,
I want to choose the place of death
That befits my dreams:
A small house,
My books,
My coffee,
And my smokes.
I am the uncertain…
But I learned
That life and death,
Like us in these lands,
Are handcuffed
From birth until death.
. . .

و لأنّي لم أختر مكان الولادة
أريد أن أختار مكاناً للممات
يليق بأحلامي:
بيتٌ صغير
كتبي
قهوتي
و بعض سجائر
أنا الحائر
خَبِرتُ أنَّ الموت و الحياة
مثلنا في هذي البلاد
مقرنين بالأصفاد
منذ الولادة
و حتى الممات
...

I am as burdened as *Atlas*,
Searching for redemption
Holding the dreams of all corpses
That filled the Mediterranean sea of death
From the seabed reaching the sky.
I am as burdened as *Atlas*.

. . .

The historiographer asks,
What is your name, tell me?
For if you come out of this sea,
You will be victorious,
I say:
I am the *Atlas* of this sea
I was not born to be victorious
But to ride the impossible
And stay here, in the nowhere,
Restructuring my past,
Waiting in the blue unseen. . .

حمّال أثقال أنا
يفتّش عن خلاص
حَمَلتُ أحلامَ كل الجثث التي
مَلَئت بحر الموت المتوسط
من القاع حتى السما
حمّال أثقال أنا

. . .

و يسألني المؤرخ
ما اسمك أنت، قل لي؟
فإن خرجت من هذا البحر انتصرت
قلت:
أنا أطلس هذا البحر
لم أولد لأنتصر
بل لأركب المستحيل
و أبقى في اللامكان هنا،
أعيد ترتيب ماضيّ
و في زُرْقة الغيب أنتظر. . .

I am as burdened as *Atlas*,
Holding the earth of the dead
On my shoulder
I am all of them,
As they are, me.

. . .

حمَّال أثقال أنا

حَمَلتُ على ظهري

أرضاً من الموتى

أنا كلُّهم

و هُمُ أنا

. . .

Where did you come from?
I came from the sea,
That was filled with corpses,
Corpses that are not different in colour,
Lying there in the seabed,
Like bullets strip.
How did they die? He asked
I thought and said,
The conscience of people is in slumber . . .
. . .
Silence
. . .

من أين أتيت؟

آتٍ من البحر الذي ملؤوه جماجم

لا فرق في ألوانها

فكلنا كمشطِ رصاصٍ

في القاع جاثم

قال: كيف ماتوا؟

قلت:

ضمير الناس نائم . . .

. . .

صمت

. ..

I came out of the sea of death, defeated.
I have my pain and a light hope.
I am waiting among the autumnal trees.
Like them,
I am devoid of all feelings I was familiar with.
The earth rolls out the yellow carpet,
Celebrating the coming of another fatigued,
Fallen like all other leaves around him.
Death has left nothing of his beginnings,
And memories are storming towards the end
. . .
Silence
. . .

خرجت من بحر الموت مهزومًا
معي ألمي و أملٌ خفيف
أنتظر بين أشجار الخريف
أنا مثلها،
مجرد من كل ما ألفت من مشاعر
تفرش الأرض لي بساطًا أصفرًا
احتفاءً بقدوم متعب آخر
سقط كلكل الأوراق حوله
لم يبق الموت أثرًا للبداية
و الذكريات تَعصِفُ بالنهاية
. . .
صمت
. . .

I am the angst of thought
And the agony of heart.
I am entering the building now
Walking slowly amidst people,
Who are indulging in affluence,
I am etherised back to a sordid life,
Worse than death.
Standing in the courtyard of an elevated, sumptuous
war museum,
Like reminiscence of a statue of an extinct human
On which is inscribed
'Thus wars do' . . .

أنا قلَقُ الفكر
و غَصَّةُ قلب
أدخل المبنى الآن
أمشي على مهلٍ
بين زحام ناس مُترَفين
كأنني من الموت عائد.
واقف في فناءِ متحفِ حربٍ رفيعٍ باذخٍ
كبقايا تمثالٍ لإنسانٍ بائد
كُتب عليه
كذا تفعل الحرب. . .

Speak

Speak, they said,
Aren't you satisfied? What do you want more?
All people of the world are speaking for you!
You are the centre!
They left the cups of wine in the night of Sunday
And they swore to stand by you for good, and forever,
And to follow your steps and feel with the sensitivity
Of their skin and with patience,
All gravels and embers on your road,
Barefoot, like you,
And to melt their flesh with their blood,
And walk on the mud,
On the frost of life,
And they swore not to betray you or leave you
On the brink of death,
Between the jaws of a guillotine,
Or be used to – God forbid – see your redolent blood,
You, the unshod, the unseen,
And they said: *you are the question*

تكلَّم

قالوا تكلَّم
أما يُرضيك؟ ماذا تريد؟
كل ألسنة الأرض استدارت في مدارك،
أنت محورها
تركوا كؤوس الخمرِ في ليلِ الأحد
و أقسموا أن ينصروك إلى الأبد و إلى الأبد
،و أن يمشوا على خطاك و أن يتحسسوا بمرهف الجِلْدِ و الجَلَد
كل حصىً و جمرٍ دربك
حافيي القدمين مثلك،
و مثلك، سيخلطون صلصالهم بدمائهم
ويمشون على الطين،
في صقيع العمر مثلك
و أقسموا أن لا يخذلوك أو يتركوك على شفى الموت
بين شقَّي مقصلة
أو تعتاد أعينهم، معاذ الله، على دمك الزَّكي، أنت الحَفِيُّ، الخَفِيّ
و قالوا أنت المسألة

And they will turn the destitution of your oppression
to affluence,
On Sunday.
So tomorrow you will forget all about the suffering of
years of oppression
If you know!
So, speak!
. . .

Come on, speak,
We have filled all the walls of websites with
Mottos, prayers, the chosen and archaic,
The beautiful and desired.
They disbelieved in your skin all those who called you a
subaltern!
Scream in all your capacity of anger
Resist with your roaring voice the barrel of the gun.
. . .

و سيحوِّلون عِجافَ قهرك لرغد
يوم الأحد
فغدًا ستنسى كل ما عانيت من قهر السنين
إن كنت تعلم
هيَّا تكلم
. . .

هيَّا تكلم
قد ملأنا كل جدران المواقع
بالشعارات، بالدعاء، بالغريب المنتقى
بالجميل المشتهى
كفروا بجلدك كل من سَمَّوْكَ تابع
اصرخ بكل ما أوتيت من غضبٍ
قاوم بصوتك الرعديدِ فوهة المدافع
. . .

Come on, speak
Don't you know?
That the minds and hearts of our cell-phones, like you, sob in prayers
And speak in the beautiful *Fusha* and beseech heaven
And some take it easy and speak in the vernacular
And others, out of their extreme sincerity, forget to speak and falter,
While you are motionless, lying on the wood, looking at the sky
And everybody was 'progressing' backwards
And you know
So, speak
. . .

هيا تكلم

ألست تعلم؟

أن عقول جوالاتنا و قلوبها تجهش مثلك بالدعاء

و تستفيض بأجمل الفصحى و تستجدي السماء

فذا يركب السهل السلس، عاميُّ الرجاء،

و ذا لفرط الصِّدق، غصَّ بدمعه، نَسِيَ الكلام، تلعثم

و أنت هامدٌ، مسجىً على خشبٍ، و تنظر للسماء

و كلٌّ تقدم للوراء

و أنت تعلم

هيا تلكم

. . .

He did not speak;

So all entered the tunnel of dejection

And everyone apart covered themselves with a cloud

All his wounds, the wounds of the earth, scream in blood

But no answer

People got bored of the image of ruins

And all cried: what is all this monotony?!

And they said:

You are the problem!

And they swore to bury you and leave you for good, forever.

. . .

Silence

. . .

لم ينطق،
دخل الجميع في نفق الكآبة
و كلٌ على حدةٍ تدثّرَ في سحابة
كلّ جراحه، جراح الأرض، تصرخ دمًا
لكن لا إجابة
ملّت الناسُ من صور الدّمار
صاح الكلُّ ما هذي الرتابة؟
و قالوا أنت المشكلة
و أقسموا أن يدفنوك و يتركوك إلى الأبد و إلى الأبد
. . .
صمت
. . .

Now you could hear nothing but the sounds of goblets
They said that they were tired of the madness of death,
This Basus war.
Sadness burdened them, heart and mind,
And everyone ended their speech with:
'May God save us'
'May God save us'

لا تسمع الآن إلا موسيقى الكؤوس
قالوا تعبنا من جنون الموت، من حرب البسوس
الحزن أثقل قلوبهم و عقولهم
و كلّهم أنهى كلامه:

"نسأل الله السلامة"
"نسال الله السلامة"

Salam (Peace)

Even if your wound bleeds forever,
Do not beg anyone.
And forever
Do not wait for anyone
To listen to your complaint.
And forever
There are, in the crowd of stabs,
Those who could not speak
And those who dance
To the tune of your wounded moans,
And those who curse the rainy clouds,
In the parched land, forever.
And forever,
There are those who hang the doves
With a strand of twisted rope . . .
But, if, one day, you are asked,
What do you want?
Say, and forever say,
I want peace . . .

سلام

و إن استمرَّ نزفُ جرحك للأبد
لا، لا تستجدِ أحد
و إلى الأبد
لا تنتظر أن يسمع الشَّكوى أحد
و إلى الأبد
هناك في زحمة الطعنات
من لا يجيد الكلام
هناك من يرقص على أنّات جرحك
و هناك في الأرض اليباب
من يلعنون الغمام إلى الأبد
و إلى الأبد
هناك من يشنقون الحمام
بحبلٍ من مَسَد . . .
لكن، إن قيل لك يوماً ما تريد؟
قل، و إلى الأبد،
أريد السلام . . .

On the Maps of Death

A migrant, sinks, in the darkness of the sea
In a silence, fully eloquent,
Forgetting all dreams . . .
Searching in the maze of memory
For the last words . . .
Uttered to one's beloved, before leaving.
Words he would not be able to utter
Engulfed in the waves
While her name, spoken in bubbles,
Completes the work of death
. . .

She is used to his absence,
For he is alive in absence . . .
If she is the shape of the word,
He is the sound–
Forms of solitude . . .
Forgotten, on the maps of death.

على خرائط الموت

مهاجرٌ يغرق في ظلمة البحر
في صمتٍ كامل التبيين
ينسى أحلامه
يبحث في تيه الذاكرة عن آخر كلماتٍ
قالها لمن أحبَّ قبل الفَوْت
كلمات لن يستطيع أن يتهجاها
يبتلعها الموج
و اسمها يخرج فقاعات من فمه
يُكمِّل عَمَلَ الموت
. . .

هي أَلِفَتِ الغياب
هو حيٌّ في غيابه . . .
هي رسم الكلمة
هو وقع الصوت . . .
أشكالٌ من العزلة
منسِيَّةٌ على خريطةِ الموت.

In Calcutta

In Calcutta,
I was not a stranger
For she charmed me into believing that I was not
In spite of the contradictions
That linger in me.
She said,
Here, you are neither a stranger
Nor a victim.
Look, you see Tagore with his Arabian *jubbah*
His body and soul wandering in it,
Flying, like a swallow, among the flocks of doves,
Residing in a space between two places,
The home and the World
. . .

في كلكتا

في كلكتا،
لم أكن غريبًا
لأنها سحرتني و صدقت أنني لست الغريب
رغم كل التناقضات
التي تسكن فيَّ
قالت:
هنا، أنت لست غريبًا،
أنت لست الضحيَّة،
انظر، ترى طاغور بجبَّته العربيَّة
بروحه و كذا الجسد
في المدينة هائم
طائر كالسنونو بين أسراب الحمائم
راقد بين المنزلين
الوطن و العالم
. . .

Oh Calcutta,

How similar you are to Damascus and her charm

In your streets, alleys,

Old shops,

In the residues of history that are still

Clamorous in the heart of the city.

In its restless quest to be the paradise of freedom,

Of art,

Of life.

. . .

كلكتا،

كم تشبهين دمشق و سحرها

في شوارعك و الحواري

في الدكاكين القديمة

في بقايا التاريخ التى لم تزل صاخبة

في صدر المدينة

في سعيها المجنون لتكون فردوس الحريَّة،

حريَّة الفن،

حريَّة الحياة

. . .

In Calcutta,
I learnt not to fold my wings,
But fly in the infinite space
In spite of injustice and darkness,
In spite of the stormy winds,
That uprooted the roots.
In spite of reckless death,
That storms from all directions.
In Calcutta, I learnt
How to resist injustice and death,
How to fight for every breath . . .

في كلكتا،
تعلمت أن لا أطوي جناحيَّ
و أطير في الفضاء اللانهائيّ
رغم الظُلم و الظَلَام
رغم الرياح العاصفة
التي اقتلعت الجذور
رغم الموت الذي يعصف
من كل الجوانب
في كلكتا تعلمت
كيف أقاوم الظلم و الموت
كيف أحارب . . .

An Exile's Whisper

The last exile whispers to the exiled:
You will not return to your soil
With which you played
On which you walked,
Unshod and carefree.
Under the olive trees,
That your father nurtured,
Along with you.
You will not return to your land
On which you uttered your first alphabet
And learned to read and write.
And raise an imagination
That adorned you.
You will not return to your mother
Who is still awaiting you,
And who, in spite of all reasons of hopelessness,
Is still holding on to frail hope.
You will not return. . .
You will not return. . .
So why don't you call me home?

همسُ منفى

يهمسُ المنْفَى الأخير للمَنْفِيّ:
لن تعود إلى التراب الذي لعبت به
و مشيت عليه
حافي القدمين
خفيف الخطى و الظِّلّ
تحت شجر الزيتون
التي دلَّلَها أبوك و دلَّلَك
و لن تعود الى الأرض التي نطقتَ بها
أولى حروفك
و تعلمت القراءة و الكتابة
و رَبَّيْتَ فيها الخيال الذي جمَّلك
لن تعود لأمِّك
هي لم تزل تنتظرك
رغم كل أسباب اليأس تؤمِّلك
لن تعود . . .
لن تعود . . .
فلماذا لا تسمني وطنك؟

The Blossom of Freedom

Eyes shimmer seeing one's being,
That is now fully complete.
Tears of joy wash the dust of the long and harsh years of waiting. . .
Trembling hands touch the gist of this existence,
Crossing the borders,
The borders of a body in which
The soul was for so long simmering,
Like burning incense . . .
A faltering voice says, 'I love you, in spite of me'. . .

Oh, the blossom of my freedom,
If you are my exile,
So to whom shall I return?!
To whom shall I return?!
To which home shall I return?!

زهرة الحرية

عيونٌ تتلألأ لرؤية ذاتها
و اكتمال الوجود
دموعُ فرحٍ تغسل غبارَ سنين انتظار صَعُوْد
رعشة يدٍ تتلمس خلاصة هذا الوجود
تعبر الحدود،
حدود جسدٍ طالما
احترقت الرّوح فيه، كما العود.
تلعثم صوتٍ يقول: "أُحِبُّكِ، رَغْمَ أنفي" . . .

يا زهر الحرية،
إن كنتِ أنتِ منفاي،
فإلى من أعود؟!
إلى من أعود؟!
إلى أيِّ وطنٍ أعود؟!

Mahmoud Al-Zayed

A Chameleon's Tale

A chameleon told me:
I do not remember the colour
With which I was born.
But I was told that I am brown,
And I became what they wanted me to be . . .
I know not the mirror,
But the surface of the lake
Tells me each time
Of a certain colour of mine:
I am, in the morning, green,
At noontime, yellow,
And in the evening,
My body is a mélange of colours.
And in the night - how lovely is the night,
I become black!
However, all the time they pass by, greeting,
They choose to see only brown,
And only brown!

قالتْ ليَ الحرباء

قالتْ ليَ الحرباء:
لا أذكرُ اللون الذي ولدتُ فيه
لكنْ قيلَ لي أنني بُنِّيَّةُ اللون
و كنت كما أرادوني أَن أكون. . .
لا أعرفُ المرآة
لكنَّ وجه البحيرةِ يخبرني
كل حينٍ بلون:
في الصباح خضراء
و في الظهيرة صفراء
و أرسم الألوان لوحةً على جسدي
عند المساء
و في الليل، كم أحب الليل،
أصير سوداء!
لكنَّهم و كلَّما مرُّوا من هنا، أَلقوا التَّحية
و قالوا: أنت بُنِّيَّة!
أنت بُنِّيَّة!

Perhaps

Life is being assassinated here
Perhaps for a rift occurred in the geography of
memory;
Maybe, if we stay thus,
We produce befuddled generations,
Generations that bury and revive history
In tune with roaring, unjust narratives . . .
Perhaps, a day will come when we will all flee to death
Why not?! . . .
For every day, a poet is being slaughtered . . .

Perhaps . . .
Perhaps the flocks of swallows will not return,
They may get expelled from their exile
And what remains for them is the borderland!
Perhaps all the wheat fields escape from us
And so do all the flocks of doves
For we forget crimes . . .
And we get forgotten . . .
For we left no place for art . . .

ربَّما

ربَّما تُغْتال الحياة هنا
لشرخٍ حدث في جغرافيا الذاكرة
ربَّما، إن بقينا هكذا، ننتج أجيالاً مربكة حائرة
تَدْفنُ التاريخ و تحييهِ
على موسيقى سردياتٍ هادرةٍ جائرة . .
ربَّما يأتي يومٌ كلُّنا فيه إلى الموت ننزح
لمَ لا؟!. . .
ففي كل يوم شاعرٌ يُذْبح . . .

ربَّما. . .
ربَّما أسراب السُّنونو لن تعود
و لربَّما تُنْفى من المنفى
وتبقى لها أرض الحدود!
ربَّما تهربُ حقول القمحِ منَّا
و كذا كل أسراب الحمائم
لأننا ننْسى الجرائم . . .
و نُنْسى . . .
لأننا لم نُبْقِ للفنِّ مطرح . . .

In Love, We Are Two Bubbles

I am the real and the imagined!
I mean, I am you. . .
And what you think I am . . .
You are you . . .
And we are both in-between:
Two bubbles flying in the space of freedom
Two bubbles escaping the gravity
Two bubbles we chase to catch
We run,
        jump,
                play
                        and get tired . . .
The two bubbles are of our making
But over them we have no control
We are the maker and the made
And in love we are two bubbles:
Fallen in love but did not touch the earth
Fallen in love but yet to reach the sky.

في الحب نحن فقاعَتان

أنا الحقيقي و المتخيَّل
و أعني أنَّني أنتِ
و ما تظنين أِنيّ أَنِيّ . . .
و أنتِ أنتِ . . .
و كلانا بين بين:
فقاعتان حلَّقَتا في فضاء الحُرِّيَّة
فقاعتان هربتَاْ من الجاذبية
نلحقها، نريد أن نمسكها
نركض،
نقفز،
نلعب،
و نتعب . . .
الفقاعتان صنعْتَنا
و لكن لا نملك من الأمر شيَّا
نحن الصانِعَاْن، المصنوعَاْن
و في الحبِّ نحن فقاعتان
وقعتا في الحب و لم تلمسا الأرض
وقعتا في الحب و لمَّا تلمسا السَّماء بعد.

Obscurity

The clearer we are with each other,
The more we become obscure
We are very obscure
For we are so clear,
Looking at the sun in the middle of summer,
Yet we are blinded by its intensity.

The more we understand the interior,
And reach the apex of understanding
The deeper language takes us down
Into the abyss of delusion
So,
The more obscure we are,
The clearer we become.
. . .

غموض

كلَّما ازددنا وضوحًا ،
ازداد غموضنا أكثر
غامضون نحن جدًّا
لأنّ وضوحنا أكبر
نرمق الشمس بصيف
و ما لنا إلا العمى . . .

كلَّما فهمنا الباطن أكثر
و وصلنا ذروةَ الفهم
أخذتنا اللغة بعيدًا بعيدًا
في هاوية الوهم،
لذا
كلَّما ازددنا غموضًا،
ازداد وضوحنا أكثر
. . .

Though we know,
Both of us know,
That silence is much more beautiful,
And we know
Both of us know
That absence is hauntingly sublime.
And we love,
Both of us love,
To play with the concepts of space and time.
Yet we always say:

Let us betray silence and speak . . .
Let us betray absence and meet . . .

رغم أنَّنا نعرف
كلانا يعرف
أنَّ الصَّمت جميل
و نعرف
كلانا يعرف
أنَّ الغياب سام
و نحن نحبُّ
كلانا يحبُّ
أن يلعب بفكرتي الزمان و المكان
دائما نقول:

لنخون الصمت و نتكلم . . .
و نخون الغياب و نلتقي . . .

The Thirtieth Year

You know that you have reached halfway
between the two childhoods of heart,
in a one-way street.
Now, you stand in the no-place, alone,
stranger, stranger,
stranger even on the land of your body.
. . .
And for the present is trees of vandalised gravestones
the war watered with the blood of the innocent,
while the earth is chewing fresh corpses
and the bodies of armament fill the sky,
you want to return . . .
to reveal your secrets to the absence,
to a woman whom you loved and left,
you want to return to wipe her tears and say:
I want you to fill this void,
so that we can walk together,
like two absent bodies,
towards another absence,
for nothing but to complete this road together.

في الثلاثين

تعرف أنك قد قطعت نصف المسافة
بين طفولتي القلب،
في شارع أحاديِّ المسار.
تقف فيه الآن، في اللامكان، وحدك،
غريبٌ، غريب
غريبٌ حتى على أرض جسمك.
. . .
و لأنَّ حاضركَ أشجارٌ من شواهد قبورٍ محطَّمة
سقتها الحربُ من دماء الأبرياء
بينما الأرض تلوك جثثًا طريَّة
و أجرامُ السلاح تغطِّي السَّماء،
تريد الإياب. . .
لتبوح بأسرارك للغياب،
لامرأةٍ كنت حبيبها و تركتها،
تريد الإياب لتمسح دموعها و تقول:
أريدك أن تملئي هذا الفراغ،
لنمشي كجسدين غائبين، لغياب آخر،
لا لشيءٍ غير أن نكمل هذا الطريق معًا

So leap from the edge of memory
to the edge of my body
to walk together towards a boundless celestial text,
to walk together from here to my hereafter
and sleep in one grave
with no name, with no trace,
two bodies nurturing a tree
to be immortal. . .
And to say to her: could I give you the key of my mind
to sleep there, forever?
Then I would reveal my secrets to none, whatsoever.
. . .

And for the future is morsels of a skinny human
coloured with the colour of the twilight,
of madness,
and sleeping under the eyelids
you want to return
. . .

فاقفزي من حافَّة الذَّاكرة
إلى حافَّة جسدي
لنسير معًا نحو نصٍّ سماويّ الحدود
لنسير معًا من هنا إلى آخرتي
و ننام معًا في حفرة واحدة
بلا اسم بلا رسم
جسدان يطعمان شجرةً
لتصبح خالدة . . .
و تقول لها: هل لي أن أعطيك مفتاح عقلي
لتنامي فيه إلى الأبد؟
عندها لن أبوح بسِرّ لأحد.
. . .
و لأنَّ المستقبل حُطام إنسانٍ هزيلٍ
ينام تحت الجفون
ملونٌ بلون الغسق، لون الجنون،
تريد الإياب
. . .

No possible return but in your night dreams
and your imagination.
There, the chains of place would not bound you in the prison of time,
so leap from here to the no-here, to imagination
and say – so that they accept you there –
I forgot my passport
I traversed all this desert through,
and I brought a book of metaphors . . .

لا عودة إلا في أحلام نومك و الخيال

هناك، لا سلاسل للمكان تقيّدِك في سجن الوقت

فاقفز من هنا إلى اللاهنا، للخيال،

و قل كي يقبلوك هناك :

نسيت جواز سفري . . .

و قطعت كل هذي المفاز

و جئتُ بسِفرٍ من مجاز . . .

Of Waiting

Between the madness of hope
And the poise of hopelessness,
I am waiting,
Like a child wanting, with a wooden ladder,
to reach the moon.
I am waiting for a yellow autumnal leaf,
Fallen out of her hand,
Taken by the wind to where the wind wants
A leaf as free as the wind
But stuck, by chance, in the thick hair of a cypress tree
While I am, as a dusty forsaken olive tree out of war
Like everything here,
Still waiting for this leaf,
A yellow love letter. . .

عن الانتظار

بين جنون الأمل
و وقار اليأس
أنتظر، كطفل يريد بسلّم خشبيّ
وصول القمر
أنتظر ورقة خريفيَّة صفراء
سقطت من يدها
أخذتها الريح حيثما أرادت الريح
حرةٌ كما الريح لكن
علقت مصادفةً بشجرةِ سروٍ
ذات شعرٍ كثيف
بينما أنا، كزيتونةٍ مهجورةٍ مغبرَّة
بفعل الحرب، ككل شيءٍ هنا
لا زلت أنتظر هذه الورقة،
رسالة حبٍ صفراء . . .

And like a body that is being called
By the soul but never replies
While the heart cries
Sufi is the lament of love
Sufi is the lament of love
I am still waiting
But this time I am waiting for the nothingness. . .
Will I be disappointed?
. . .

While waiting,
I see the absence absencing
I see my body absencing
Before my eyes
But this time, there is no farewell
There is no hand waving for me or for him
Here is my body, I can see him before me,
A heap of withered limbs . . .
. . .

و كجسد تناديه الروح
تعال فلا يجيب،
بينما القلبُ يهتفُ:
الحبُّ صوفيٌّ النحيب
الحبُّ صوفيٌّ النحيب
لازلت أنتظر
أنتظر اللاشيء هذه المرة
فهل أخيب؟
. . .

في الانتظار
أرى الغياب يغيب
أرى جسدي أمام عينيَّ يغيب
لا وداع هذه المرة
لا يد تلوح لي أو له
أراه الآن ، هو ذا أمامي
ركام أطراف ذاوية . . .
. . .

While waiting,
I know the abyss of time,
The abyss of place,
The abyss of the self,
And the abyss of abyss itself

في الإنتظار
أعرف هاوية الوقت
و هاوية المكان
و أعرف هاوية النفس
و هاوية الهاوية

A Letter to a Silent Absence

I am, in your absence, shreds of bereaved poems,
And tired of the absence of the Euphrates and Tigris.
Will you return and end
The emptiness of solitude?
. . .

I am tired of waiting at all checkpoints,
And hopeless in this age of massacres,
Will you return and declare the birth of a poet,
And resurrect hope with your poetry,
A smile on the face of a feeble wanderer?
. . .

هل تعودين و تَشربيني قهوة
صنعتها على مَهلٍ سحابة؟
و أعرف أَنِّي أنت،
لكن أقول شِعركِ بالإنابة . . .
فهل تعودين وتكمِّلِي فعل الكتابة؟
. . .

و إن عُدْتِ،
هل تكسرينَ سلاسلَ حَبْسي
أم تنقشين قصيدة يأسي
و إن عُدتُ
هل أعود إليك
أم أعود لنفسي؟ . . .

Her Song

She, a celestial song, sang a nursery song,
a song that harkens to a bygone childhood
that is, as is his, for oblivion.
Could we keep this child surviving in us
without the indelible memories and
commands chiseled in a fatigued memory?
Could we keep the childhood of the heart alive
even when we are trapped in the intricacies of life?

She, a song of a wandering Sufi, said,
I am a poem of in-between,
transfigured in this body of mine,
and through the metamorphosis of my body,
I can sneak to your body and come back again,
without your notice, with your permission. . .

أغنيتها

هي، أغنية سماويَّة، غنَّت أغنية طفولةٍ
أغنية تعود إلى طفولة غابرة
طفولة، كطفولته، هي للنسيان . . .
هل لنا أن نحافظ على هذا الطفل فينا
من غير الأوامر و الذكريات المحفورة في ذاكرة متعبة؟
هل لنا أن نحافظ على طفولة القلب فينا
بينما نحن غارقون في تعقيدات الحياة؟

هي، أغنية صوفيٍّ هائم، قالت:
أنا قصيدةُ بين بين
تجلَّتْ في جسدي هذا
و بتحولات جسدي
أستطيع أن أتسلل إلى جسدك
و أعود ثانية من غير أن تلحظ، و أنت موافق. . .

Silence electrifies these two bodies, together, whose voluptuousness is kept numbed in the presence of new meanings in themselves.

Bodies are like ruins of language.

And as these meanings touch their bodies, the latter shudder, redden and beget words that fall from the edges of these bodies to the commotion of the language that lies in-between-their-mother-tongues, a third language carrying opaque meanings that transform these bodies into a new text:
a translated poem.

الصمت يكهربُ هذين الجسدين معًا،
فالشهوانيّة خُدِّرت في حضرةِ معاني جديدة في النفس.

أجسامٌ كحطامِ اللغة . . .

فإذا لامستها هذه المعاني
اهتزت و تورَّدت و أنجبت كلمات تسقط من حافَّة الجسدين
إلى اهتياج لغةٍ ترقد بين لغتيهما الأم،
لغة ثالثة تحمل معاني مبهمة، تحوِّل الجسدين إلى نصٍّ
جديد: قصيدة مترجمة.

Speech is their sin,
a source of inception of all misconceptions . . .
while writing, with all its silences,
translates silence and absence.
They both leap into the space of the in-between,
their free space,
to communicate solely through the written, to *be,*
to be an unforgettable translation of two absencing
bodies in the memory of time.

She asked, Could we betray absence after all this
silence?
The child in him hastily jumped and said, Yes, yes.

الكلام خطيئة

و مصدر أفهام خاطئة . . .

و الكتابة، و بكل ما تحويه من صمتٍ،

تترجم الصمت و الغياب.

فكلاهما يثب إلى هذا المكان الوسط،

فضائهما الحرّ،

ليتحدثا بالكتابة وحدها،

كي يملكوا كينونتهم:

كي يكونا ترجمةً لا تنسى لجسدين يغيبان في ذاكرة الوقت.

سَأَلتْ: هل نستطيع أن نخون الغياب بعد كل هذا الصمت؟

الطفل الذي يسكن فيه ردَّ مسرعًا: نعم، نعم

I ask myself, Why does he want to trace himself in her foreign memory and strange past?
Why does he keep her as an immortal being, planted in his memory and, hence, he is writing her though she is a foreign land? Why? . . .

The child jumped again and said, Because her song has to be written, and I have to sing it for good, forever. . .

Smiling, I now answer:
Because she created me anew;
she begot me,
and she begot me in fog
she begot me in absence.

سألتُ نفسي: لماذا يريد أن يقتفي أثر نفسه في ذاكرة أجنبية و ماض غريب؟
لماذا يريدها كائنًا لا يفنى، مزروعًا في ذاكرته و لذا يكتبها
رغم أنّها أرض أجنبيّة؟ لماذا؟. . .

وثب الطفل ثانية و قال: لأن أغنيتها يجب أن تُكتب و يجب أن أغنيها للأبد و إلى الأبد . . .

أمَّا الآن فأقول مبتسمًا:
لأنها أحالتني خَلْقًا آخر؛
لأنها ولدتني ،
و ولدتني في الضباب،
ولدتني في الغياب.

The Malady of Language

I sowed the non-being,
Watered it with the wine of sheer immortality,
Reaped nothingness in full bloom,
Hid it out of space.
Like an old and hollow tree,
In the middle of wilderness,
My heart is hollow and empty.
. . .

With all possible ferocity,
I am angry.
Angry I am,
At all this powerlessness,
At all this helplessness,
In the presence of this plague of killing
. . .

داءُ اللُّغة

زرعتُ العدم
سقيتهُ خمرَ الخلود المطلق
حصدتُ اللّاشيءَ مُكتملاً نباتُه
خبّأتهُ خارج المكان.
كشجرة عتيقةٍ جوفاء
وسط البيداء
قلبي فارغٌ أجوف
...

غاضبٌ أنا
بكل ما أوتيت من شراسة
غاضبٌ أنا
من كل هذا العجز
من كل هذا اليأس
أمام طاعون القتل
...

With all possible insanity,
Angry I am,
And with all possible impetuosity,
I want in a second,
To swallow the earth, the sky,
The sun, the moon,
And all the rest of stars and planets.
And in the stupor of killing
Revolving around me,
I declare,

I do not belong to this earth, this slaughterhouse.

My original sin is writing poetry.
My last sin is writing poetry.
And in the presence of all this mass killing,
All this pain,
I want to define the non-being
I want to understand the beginning,
For I may have power over the end.
I will produce words unspoken,

غاضب أنا
بكل ما أوتيت من جنون
أريد للحظةٍ، و بكل ما مُلئت من نَزَقٍ
أن أبلعَ الأرض و السماء
و الشمس و القمر
و ما تَبقَّى من نجوم و كواكب
و في سكرة القتل من حولي،
أُعلنُ:

أنا لا أنتمي إلى هذي الأرض، المذبحة.

خطيئتي الأولى أنني أكتب الشعر
و خطيئتي الآخرة أنني أكتب الشعر
ففي حضرة كل هذا الهرج
كل هذا الألم
أريد تعريف العدم
أريد أن أعرف البداية
لأملك النهاية
سآتي بمفردات لم تقل

Images undrawn
And a sublime metaphor, unreachable.
And in the presence of the brutal commonplace
guillotine
I search for feelings, non-trivial.
All that is repeated is doomed to be boring
All that is absent is doomed to be desired.
I want to come up with a new language,
Signaling a new dawn,
Breathing without the stench of blood.

لكنَّني . . .
أعترف الآن أمامكم
أنَّني أعاني من داءٍ عضالٍ
إنَّه داءُ اللغة:
فشلٌ في أن أترجم المشاعر
و فشلٌ في أن أترجم الفكر
هل هناك عذاب أسوأ
من أن تحاصر بعجزين:
عجزٌ عن الفعل في حضرة القتل
و عجزٌ في صَنْعَةِ اللغة
. . .

I am the non-being
I sentenced myself to repeat the attempt,
And I was sentenced with failure for years.
Since poetry seduced me
And I accepted the rule of seduction,
I have become a rebel,
And named myself a poet,
Fusing the beginning with the end. . .

أنا العدم

حكمت على نفسي بتكرار المحاولة

و محكوم عليَّ بالفشل منذ سنين

مذ راودني الشعر عن نفسي

و قبلت قانون الغواية

صرت ثائرًا

و سميت نفسي شاعرًا،

دامجًا البداية بالنهاية . . .

What is the Use of Poetry After Carnage?

What is the use of the wheat of poetry
If it covers all the heights of lands,
While the sky drops upon them
Pieces of all kinds of arms?
What is the use of the ears of poetry
If they cover the fields of the body,
Her body, while they forget and
Conceal all scars of the wounds?. . .
What is the use of poetry, all poetry,
If it covers the face of this earth, this graveyard.
What is the use of poetry after carnage?

ما نفع الشِّعر بعد المجزرة؟

ما نفع قمح الشّعر
إن ملأ كل أعالي البلاد
بينما السَّماءُ تسَّاقط عليها
كِسَفًا من كل أنواع السلاح؟
ما نفع سنابل الشّعر
إن ملأت حقول الجسد،
جسدها، و نست
و أخفت كل آثار الجراح؟. . .
ما نفع الشّعر، كل الشّعر
إن غطّى وجه الأرض،
هذي المقبرة؟
ما نفع الشّعر بعد المجزرة؟

Absencing

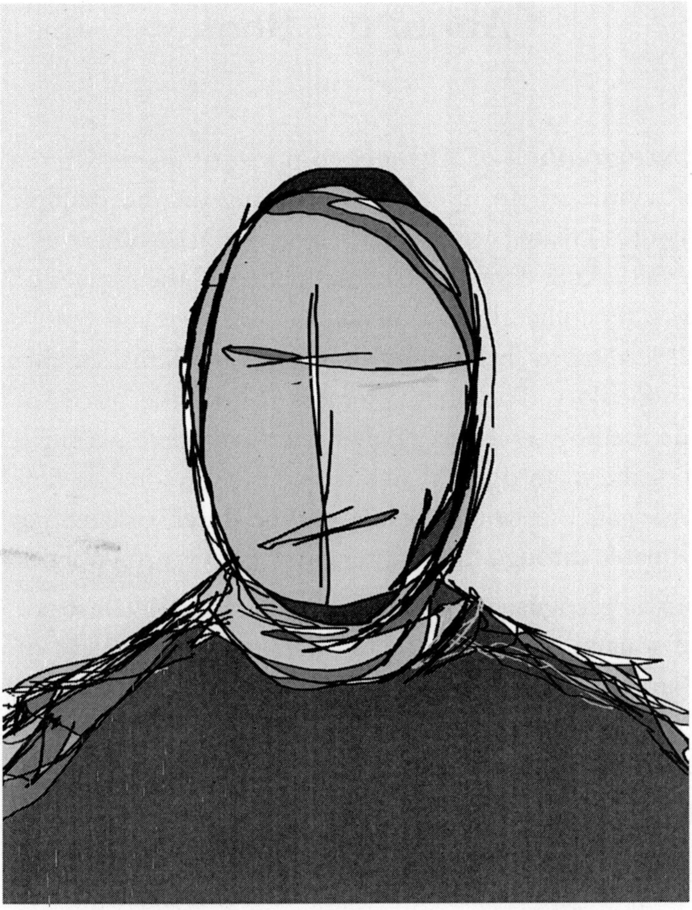

Absence

Mahmoud Al-Zayed

About the Book

Cartographies of Absence comprise of poems written at a time of an upheaval – focusing on the multiple fissures created within the self and within others as a result of the cumulative consequence of the ravages of war, repetitive displacements, loss of love and faith – all leading to 'bell-jarring' life to a few sterile samples of memory. The poet, attempts to join the pieces of the memory-collages by giving it a collective narrative. Yet, the form doesn't stick to the conventional as time and again the 'wound' resurfaces and the chaos becomes palpable through the disintegrated yet powerful poetics.

History, language, love, identity, geographical 'construct' of a nation, death – nothing misses the mind's eye of the poet. By focusing on their 'absences' the poet in his own way, rebels against the act of burying them in oblivion. This forms the corpus of the text.

The intensity of the poems, is to some extent, mellowed by the phonetic musicality of the Arabic text, which serves as an interesting complement to the fragmented pieces written in English, creating harmonious poetic ensembles. This contrapuntal play of Arabic and English texts safely posits its place of the 'in-between', not just in the case of its content, but also of the fluidity of two languages making the narrative one of a kind.

About the Author

Mahmoud Al-Zayed is the author of *Cartographies of Absence*. Born and raised in Tayyibat al-Imam, Hama, Syria, he is a researcher, translator, and poet. As an ICCR scholar, he completed his doctoral research from the Department of English, Jamia Millia Islamia, New Delhi, India. An avid reader and writer, this book marks his debut in making his poetry public, which have been in the remnants of his private space since long.

As an academic scholar, he has been part of many national and international seminars/conferences discussing the discourses of 'resistance' in literature and cinema.

Mahmoud Al-Zayed